Identifying and Solving Problems:
a system approach

Third Edition

Roger Kaufman

UNIVERSITY ASSOCIATES, INC.

8517 Production Avenue, P.O. Box 26240
San Diego, California 92126

Cover design and illustrations by Patrick Murgillo

Copyright © 1976, 1979, 1982 by International Authors, B.V.
ISBN: 0-88390-050-5
Library of Congress Catalog Card Number: 76-5702
Printed in the United States of America

preface to the third edition

Life used to be much simpler than it is now; we were able to sense a problem, cleverly suggest a solution, and then go ahead and do what we had chosen to do.

When the world was not as complex—and when there were fewer demands made on our human and financial resources—the trainer, manager, counselor, or consultant could easily relate means and ends. But now we have to be especially careful about linking what we do, why we do it, and how we get the job done, in order to better assure ourselves and our associates that what we set out to do is what we should accomplish.

Earlier editions of this book focused on a basic, six-step process for identifying and resolving problems. This tool continues to be useful today and it appears in this third edition.

The second edition described the internal and external aspects of an organization and noted that there are five organizational elements that, when related correctly, can allow us to identify organizational problems and relate them to societal impact. This frame of reference—the "Organizational Elements Model"—is further developed in this volume.

From working with people such as yourself, we have gained knowledge about what it takes to be a successful consultant, human resource developer, trainer, manager, or executive: it requires correctly linking and justifying organizational efforts, organizational results, and societal impact. This third edition adds material on the organizational elements model (or "big picture" of organizational efforts, results, and impact) that is useful in identifying needs as well as on the procedures for step-by-step determination of problems and how to resolve them. Thus, we are building from former editions and concepts to the ways in which both these tools may be useful to you in identifying, justifying, and solving problems. Together they form a SYSTEM APPROACH.

Our title is the same, but the development and explanation of each tool has been expanded, clarified, and integrated. This edition—as the two before it—is designed to help you help yourself to be more successful, regardless of whether you are a trainer, consultant, executive, human resource developer, manager, or something other. This book is intended to provide you with a blueprint for identifying and solving problems.

Acknowledgments

Many people have contributed toward making this book useful and helpful. These include graduate students and colleagues at Florida State University and United States International University, professors and students at other institutions, and many, many readers and users of the first two editions—people in business, the military, education, and public service.

I specifically would like to thank the staff of the Center for Needs Assessment and Planning at Florida State University, including Bob Stakenas, Michael Knight, Kelly Watson, Bruce Stone, and Hanna Mayer. Also, I would like to thank Leon Lessinger, Harold Greenwald, Ted Blau, Bob Morgan, Bob Mager, Joe Mills, Leon Simms, Fen English, Andrew Carron, Alice Grow, Jan Grau, Jean Van Dyke, Arlette Ballew, Merilyn Britt, and Jan Kaufman.

Special thanks to Bob Stakenas for intellectual challenges and mental refreshment, and to Patrick Murgillo for helping to make this message come alive with his expert illustrations and design.

Roger Kaufman

Tallahassee, Florida
January, 1982

contents

one

understanding means & ends

NEEDS AND WANTS—
AN IMPORTANT DIFFERENCE

Sometimes people want us to "buy" their solution before we *really* know what the problem is. That's what those headlines on the previous page are all about.

People say they "need" luxuries, products, programs, services—all kinds of things they don't have.

But do they believe that these things will *fulfill* NEEDS or do they think they *are* NEEDS?

That's more than just an idle question.

We can save

MONEY

TIME

HUMAN RESOURCES

IF we can stop jumping into solutions before we are sure what our problem is.

NEEDS and wants are *not* the same. Nor are problems and solutions the same!

PICTURE THIS SCENE:

Let's take a closer look at this.

I "need" a new Rolls Royce convertible.

Just WHY does our friend want (or desire or require):

A CAR, and/or

A NEW car, and/or

A new Rolls convertible car?

And while we're at it, why, particularly, use the word "need" in the statement?

Maybe someone is trying to "sell" something as a necessity or an imperative when it *really* isn't!

Maybe a new Rolls is just one of several alternatives (or options) for meeting the real NEED.

It might help to divide things into two piles:

MEANS and ENDS

And see how that works for our car example.

MEANS	ENDS
Feet Bicycle Scooter Motorcycle Camper truck Economy car	Transportation for work and pleasure
Rolls Royce Mercedes Sailing yacht Private plane	Status

It is obvious that most of the time when we use the word NEED, we jump right over other possible MEANS (or options) and

LOCK OURSELVES IN . . .

to a solution that might not be the best one to reach the desired END.

Somehow many of us confuse **MEANS AND ENDS**

when we use the word NEED as a verb. Instead, we should use NEED only to describe a gap between a current result and a desired result.

We often jump to premature solutions and get into problems over our heads.

We should select our MEANS based on the ENDS we wish to achieve.

DANGER QuickSAND

Well, at least he'll avoid the snake.

Look at the confusion everywhere . . .

These opinions really are solutions . . .

in search of a problem.

Although well-intentioned, many solutions that people offer are not linked to important ENDS . . .

And when MEANS and ENDS are not linked sensibly, we often fail—even with the best of intentions!

Let's not confuse **MEANS and ENDS!**

Because that's a lot of work to go nowhere.

Let's use the *same words* for the same things!
Here are some definitions:

END: The result: OUTCOME, OUTPUT, or PRODUCT . . .

MEANS: The tools, methods, techniques, or PROCESS used to achieve an END . . .

NEED: The gap between current results (or ENDS) and desired results (or ENDS) . . .

> (Notice that NEED is a noun, *not* a verb; nor is it used in the *sense* of a verb.)

PROBLEM: A NEED selected for closure; a gap to be closed . . .

Let's see how these definitions can work for us.

> The customers (81 percent) of a bank say, "We 'need' longer banking hours."

> The vice presidents (77 percent) say, "We 'need' shorter banking hours."

> Tellers (67 percent) say, "We 'need' higher pay."

Look like a conflict? Maybe not—perhaps each group has confused MEANS and ENDS and jumped right to solutions (higher pay, shorter hours, etc.) without defining the NEED as the gap between current results (or ENDS) and desired results.

NEEDS versus wants . . . isn't that semantic quibbling?

It isn't if it results in our <u>not</u> correctly solving our important problems!

Let's see what each group is saying in terms of MEANS and ENDS.

MEANS	ENDS
Customers: longer banking hours	?
Vice Presidents: shorter banking hours	?
Tellers: more money	?

No ENDS or results are stated! We only can infer them.

Before rushing into any solution (even if someone calls it a NEED), we first should define and justify the ENDS to be accomplished. It really makes more sense to decide *how* to do something after we know *what* we are to accomplish.

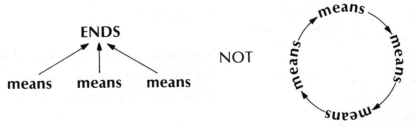

Let's see . . .

Try to sort some of the "hot" issues in contemporary living into MEANS and ENDS.

	MEANS	ENDS
Welfare		
Abortion		
Open-choice education		
Supply vs. demand economics		
Decreased government spending		
Preserving the environment		
Increased defense budget		

Do all these turn out to be solutions in search of problems?

Will these MEANS produce desired ENDS? Do proposers of MEANS link their solutions to desired results—or do they just hope that they will be useful?

The issues listed above *all* are MEANS!

If you're not part of the solution, you're part of the problem.

Let's begin by defining terms. Perhaps we do not know the real problem!

We can argue almost forever about MEANS—

- IF we don't know what we want to accomplish
  (and why we want to accomplish it).

- IF we don't define the appropriate ENDS, or OUTCOMES.

> "A poorly defined problem
> may have an infinite
> number of solutions."

Whoever said that must
have worked in my office.

We propose that you can be more

```
┌─────────────────────┐
│                     │
│     EFFECTIVE       │
│        and          │
│     EFFICIENT       │
│        and          │
│     HUMANE          │
│                     │
└─────────────────────┘
```

. . . if you will first define (and justify) the END
before choosing the MEANS.

Shall we try it? Sort the following into MEANS and ENDS.
Which could be ENDS?

MEANS	END

Learn problem solving

Get a job

Have a positive self-concept

Join an encounter group

Teach music

Move to Bora Bora

Graduate from college

Survive

Love

Ban nuclear generators

	MEANS	END
Learn problem solving	√	
Get a job	?	?
Have a positive self-concept	?	?
Join an encounter group	√	
Teach music	?	?
Move to Bora Bora	?	?
Graduate from college	√	
Survive		√
Love	?	?
Ban nuclear generators	√	

Why all those question marks?

You've caught us.
Sometimes something is a MEANS
and sometimes it also may be an END.

Some of us want to love so that someone will love us in return,
so that we will feel secure. And we might want to get a job to
make money, to buy a car, or to graduate from college.

I'm going to Bora Bora so I don't have to get a job.

Each milestone along the way to an END can be perceived as an END in itself, or as a MEANS to a larger or more distant END.

But what is most important to the success of any venture is to make sure that there is a RECOGNIZED, DEFINED, and JUSTIFIED RESULT we are aiming for—an END to be achieved.

(Actually, in the previous list, "survive" is probably the only *basic* OUTCOME; the others really relate most to *quality of survival.*)

We must make certain that there is a well-defined distinction and relationship between MEANS and ENDS!

Consider, each time you plan something or do something, what you want to achieve, both:

- NOW, and
- LATER, as a result of this achievement.

But to keep MEANS and ENDS in perspective, ask yourself:
"IF I DO THIS, WHAT WILL BE THE RESULT?"
If it already is an END, you will know it.
If not, this approach will help keep you focused on results.

Keep asking yourself this question until you have identified the END. You then will have shifted focus from MEANS to ENDS . . . from solutions to problems.

If I buy a new Rolls,
I will have transportation,
make the neighbors envious,
and get better treatment when
I drive up to a restaurant.

Maybe there's a better and
simpler way to get to places
and to gain esteem.

There are several kinds of results . . .
some that are desired by an organization or an individual
and some that are societal in nature.

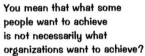

You mean that what some
people want to achieve
is not necessarily what
organizations want to achieve?

. . . but sometimes
they are the same.

Some results or ENDS are outside of (*EXTERNAL* to) the organization or the individual—they exist in society.

AND

Some results are within an organization.

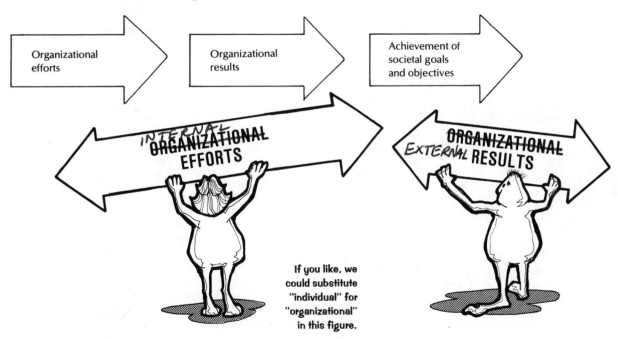

Organizational efforts

Organizational results

Achievement of societal goals and objectives

INTERNAL ORGANIZATIONAL EFFORTS

ORGANIZATIONAL EXTERNAL RESULTS

If you like, we could substitute "individual" for "organizational" in this figure.

Personal or organizational results,
to be most effective,
should be directly related to societal results—
results that are useful in and for society.

Organizations are MEANS to societal ENDS.

I like comfort and status when I drive!

Those will give him really great utility when we deplete the world resources of oil.

ALL GONE

In order to differentiate between various kinds of MEANS and ENDS, we can relate them:

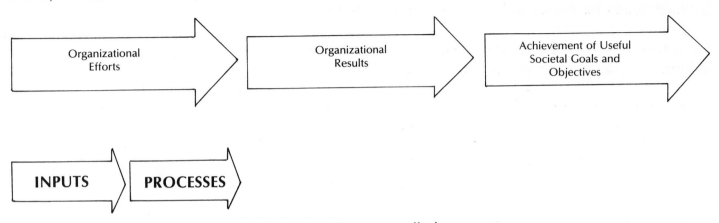

... What an organization has available for its efforts are called INPUTS; PROCESSES are "how-to-do-its" for using the INPUTS.

Both INPUTS and PROCESSES make up "Organizational Efforts."

Organizational Efforts bring results. The first type of result is PRODUCTS, the en-route accomplishments that will be the building blocks for the second type of result: OUTPUTS.

OUTPUTS are the "Organizational Results" that may be delivered to society—outside the organization.

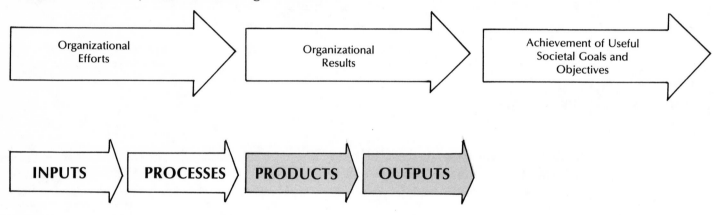

Organizational Efforts yield Organizational Results, and
Organizational Results have
IMPACT
in and for society.

The Societal Results are called OUTCOMES.

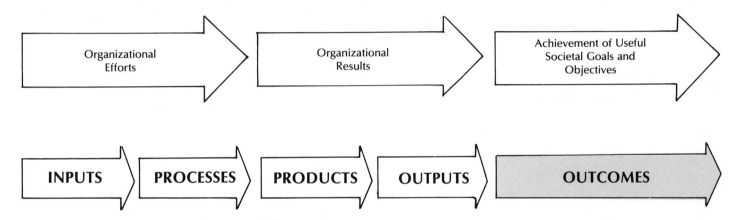

In order to differentiate between various kinds of MEANS and ENDS, we may relate them to one another this way:

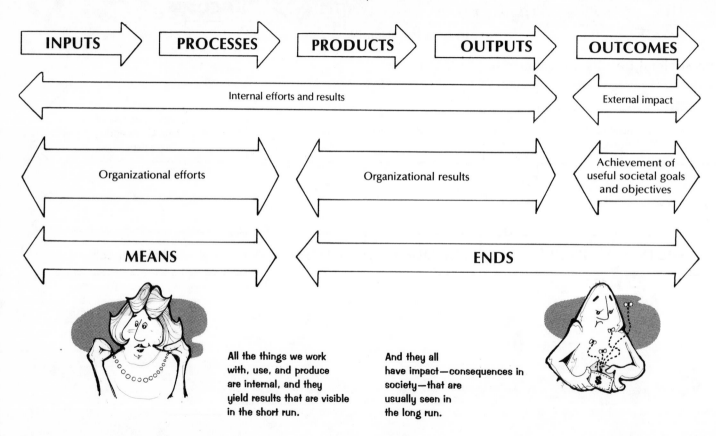

INPUTS → PROCESSES → PRODUCTS → OUTPUTS → OUTCOMES

Internal efforts and results

External impact

Organizational efforts

Organizational results

Achievement of useful societal goals and objectives

MEANS

ENDS

All the things we work with, use, and produce are internal, and they yield results that are visible in the short run.

And they all have impact—consequences in society—that are usually seen in the long run.

These five Organizational Elements, when related to one another, are called

THE ORGANIZATIONAL ELEMENTS MODEL

Its use will allow you to relate:
- MEANS and ENDS
- ORGANIZATIONAL (or personal) RESOURCES, EFFORTS, and RESULTS

. . . with success in life.

Because others around us are not always precise about the words they use, here are some useful definitions:

INPUTS are the ingredients and raw materials we have to work with—those people and things that are available and with which we start. They include our existing goals and objectives.

PROCESSES are the ways in which we use, orchestrate, and manage our INPUTS—our how-to-do-its and methods.

PRODUCTS are the en-route results we get on the way to organizational and societal results.

OUTPUTS are the total results of the organization or individual—that which is delivered or deliverable to society.

OUTCOMES are the results of all the organization's efforts, PRODUCTS, and OUTPUTS in society—they are external to the individual or organization.

Lots of words . . .

I guess it pays to separate different kinds of means and ends.

Let's look at some examples of each.

For an organization

INPUTS	PROCESSES	PRODUCTS	OUTPUTS	OUTCOMES
• money	• organization development	• tire	• yearly auto production	• more people self-sufficient and contributing
• people	• management techniques	• assembled automobiles	• automobiles sold	• reduced illness due to air pollution
• equipment	• manufacturing techniques	• divisional quota met	• stockholder vote of confidence	• reduced fatalities
• facilities	• formulas	• training manuals	• money for continuation	• quality of life improved
• goals	• training	• trained workers		• fewer welfare recipients
• time	• production line	• worker agreement		• profit
• resources	• quality control	• course completed		
• needs	• management by objective			
• problems (currently existing)	• curriculum			

For an Individual

INPUTS	PROCESSES	PRODUCTS	OUTPUTS	OUTCOMES

- money
- personality
- mental & physical characteristics
- resources
- needs
- goals
- desires
- problems (currently existing)

- critical thinking
- intuition
- guilt
- depression
- task oriented
- valuing
- problem solving
- defense mechanism
- going through psychotherapy

- monthly paycheck
- master macrame
- purchase car
- clean house
- dinner party held

- obtain first career position
- marry loved one
- graduate from college
- obtain service discharge
- maintain weight

- expenses less than income
- good physical health
- positive future prospects
- freedom from fear
- financial independence

The Organizational Elements Model is *not* linear or "lock-step."

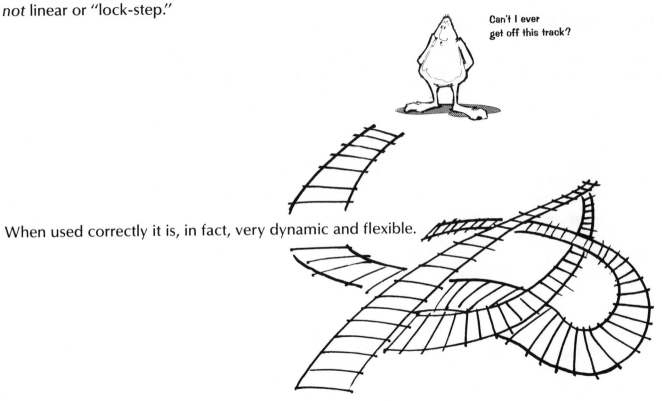

When used correctly it is, in fact, very dynamic and flexible.

Frequently, an INPUT leads to a PROCESS.

Many times a PROCESS becomes a part of another PROCESS.

INPUTS	PROCESSES	PRODUCTS	OUTPUTS	OUTCOMES
Money ———→ ①	Build train-ing program ② ↓ Try out training program ③			

Sometimes a PRODUCT may become an INPUT to be used in another PROCESS.

INPUTS	PROCESSES	PRODUCTS	OUTPUTS	OUTCOMES
Money → ①	Build train-ing program ②			
	Try out training program ③	→ Training program validated ④		
Validated training program ⑤	→ Schedule trainees ⑥			
	Conduct training ⑦	→ Trainees have required skills ⑧		

The Organizational Elements Model relates and interrelates

- MEANS and ENDS

- Organizational efforts and
  organizational results

- Organizational results and
  social (or personal) success
  and impact

- What we are to do, how we do
  it, and the results we achieve.

. . . And if you want to determine the usefulness of anything
resulting from any Organizational Element, simply determine if
it is making a useful contribution to the next Organizational
Element . . . determine if the "fit" between Organizational
Elements is appropriate.

Useful, systematic planning relates

- Internal resources, efforts, and methods

to

- Organizational (in-house) results

to

- External results

and, thus, better assures that individual and organizational efforts yield useful OUTCOMES.

OUTCOMES are results in and for society.

And we must make certain that these OUTCOMES are appropriate for Now and the Future.

If organizations, through their efforts and results, are not useful to society, they will cease to exist—sooner or later.

INPUTS, PROCESSES, and PRODUCTS all contribute to organizational results that are called OUTPUTS.

OUTPUTS (it is hoped that they are appropriate and useful) contribute to external results that are called OUTCOMES.

We always should try to achieve useful OUTCOMES— positive impact in and for society.

An OUTPUT would be a diploma, a degree, or a certificate.

An OUTCOME would be self-sufficiency: surviving and contributing in society—outside of school.

Confusing internal efforts and results
with useful external impact and utility
can bring about FAILURE—unintentionally.

We have just
broken the world
speed record!

TESTING
GROUNDS

. . . and he flew the
wrong way!
Look out
for the
mountain!

The ultimate usefulness of MEANS
(organizational efforts) *and* the
organizational results they achieve

are the

External ENDS (OUTCOMES)

All the MEANS—the INPUTS, the PROCESSES—and all the
internal results—the PRODUCTS and the OUTPUTS—are useful
only to the extent that they have utility in the real world
(*external* to the individual and the organization)!

In problem solving and decision making (whether we are parents, teachers, managers, counselors, or just plain persons), results are important.

Why don't we start right now by getting MEANS (INPUTS and PROCESSES) and ENDS (PRODUCTS, OUTPUTS, and OUTCOMES) in the correct perspective?

two

where are we going? and why?

REALISTIC GOAL SETTING

Setting goals, or clearly stating what "end" we want to achieve, is *critical*—if we really want to get from where we are to where we want to be.

The first step in realistic goal setting is to list two dimensions in **MEASURABLE TERMS.**

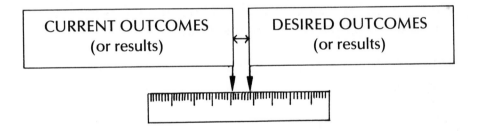

If we are now achieving certain results, and we want another result, then we **must** be precise in describing the gap or measurable discrepancy between current and desired OUTCOMES.

For example:

> *45 percent of our employees have a negative image of the company, and we want to reduce that percentage to no more than 10 percent.*

Must our statements of results be measurable?
"Must" is a strong word, but if you really want to make a difference—really to change—then the more precise you can be, the higher your probability of achieving the desired change. And making the statements relate to desired OUTCOMES will further assure the utility of the efforts.

Let's see why

MEASURABILITY

might be so

important.

Look at these two statements of "current results":

My work turns out badly and it takes me longer to do it than it takes my co-workers. I didn't get a promotion and raise when I thought I would. My supervisor always checks on me. And I think George wants my job.

I don't like where I work.

Which statement provides us with more information? Which statement seems most useful?

Which statement allows us to determine:

- WHAT RESULTS WE ARE GETTING NOW

and

- WHAT RESULTS WE WANT?

Sure, the first one is more helpful (and it is also more precise).

The more PRECISE and MEASURABLE we can be, the more chance we have of:

- Making sure we are setting meaningful and appropriate goals;

- Making appropriate choices among possible MEANS in order to get from where we are to where we want to be.

First, realize that you don't *have* to measure at all—except when you *really* want to make a difference! (If you don't care, or don't want to know if you have gone from What Is to What Should Be, then don't measure.) However . . .

If you want to change or make a change, the more precisely you measure the more you can know:

- IF YOU ARE ON THE RIGHT TRACK.

- IF YOU HAVE BEEN SUCCESSFUL.

- WHAT SHOULD BE CHANGED IF YOU ARE NOT SUCCESSFUL.

Did you say **44 long** or **34 long**?

Measurement and the devices for measurement may be likened to other tools . . . They are amoral—neither good nor evil . . .

You can use a hammer to pound someone into the ground or you can use it to build a temple. The user determines whether a tool is used appropriately.

We don't want to do away with all measurement because some people have misused measurement in the past.
Our job is USING MEASUREMENT to help ourselves and our fellow humans.

. . . And, by the way, when we measure, it doesn't have to be in terms of the familiar statistical means and standard deviations; any time we label something we are, in fact, measuring!

In fact, we know of four scales of measurement:

Nominal

Ordinal

Interval

Ratio

And we suggest that

the more refined and precise the scale of measurement, *the more reliable* the measure!

Let's see some possible uses for each.

Nominal-scale measures simply name or label:

If you can *name* something, you ARE measuring! (And if you can't at least name something, like "Love," "Beauty," "Actualization," etc., then you can't really be sure it exists!)

Ordinal-scale measurement involves ranking:

My preference list is:

1. Steak	5. Chocolate Cake
2. Lobster	6. Cherry Pie
3. Pizza	7. Hot Dog
4. Won Ton Soup	8. Pistachio Ice Cream

We can't say how much more or less preferred each item is, compared to the others. But we can rank them in order by some criterion such as personal appeal, your taste buds, or your appetite.

With this type of scale, we can say only that one thing is:

- Greater than

- Equal to

    or

- Less than
  something
  else

In everyday language we use ordinal-scale measurements frequently, such as:

Interval-scale measurements are most often associated with science and scientists, but everyone can use them…

They have equal scale distances but an arbitrary zero point. The important thing they tell us is the degree of distance from that arbitrary point, such as

- maps: the equator and the prime meridian at Greenwich are arbitrary zero points.

- thermometers: zero degrees, Fahrenheit or Centigrade, is an arbitrary zero point.

- clocks: midnight is an arbitrary zero point.

So is getting up to go to work!

We often use interval-scale measurements in planning human change; most of our psychological tests (including ones using those infernal arithmetic means and standard deviations) are interval-scale measurements.

When we want to plan change, we are best off if we use interval-scale measures or if we use . . .

Ratio-scale measurement. Measures such as feet or pounds are like interval-scale measures, except that the zero point really means "zero." It is a starting place that occurs naturally.

Minus forty pounds?
That's impossible!

Ratio-scale measures are difficult to apply usefully to human behavior, so let's concentrate on

● **Nominal** ● **Ordinal** ● **Interval**

It's inefficient to use a **less-refined** scale of measurement when we have more precise measures that are valid.

I prefer this car because it has 250 h.p., gets 30 m.p.g., and has a 40,000 mile guarantee.

I like the yellow car better than the green.

. . . Or to try to use a **too-refined** measure when that scale is inappropriate to what we are measuring.

How many micromillimeters will this plant grow in eight and a half months?

When we set our goals, we are best off if we can state our current results (or OUTCOMES) in INTERVAL-SCALE terms, the most **precise** scale that generally applies to human behavior.

I remember, "outcomes" relates to external or societal results.

Any statement of desired objectives should do the following things:

- Tell what result is to be achieved.

- Tell when the result will be achieved.

- Tell what criteria will measure its achievement and under what conditions it will be measured and by whom.

- Communicate without confusion.

And remember: the more results statements that we can make in interval-scale terms, the better will be our

PLANNING

DOING

EVALUATION

REVISION (and Renewal)

Let's look at a possible example for framing a results statement that will perform the four functions we mentioned previously . . .

By the time I am 55, and the children have graduated from college and are out on their own (so that I won't have to contribute money to them), I will be earning $45,000 a year in a job I like, our home will be paid for, my wife and I will enjoy more of life's good things, based upon a greater spendable income than now. We will each own a car. We will dine out more frequently. We will travel abroad for at least two vacations. At home we will buy season tickets to the symphony. I will have put enough money aside to purchase a small income property (under $200,000 then) for my retirement. My wife and I will be in "good health" as indicated by a licensed physician's physical examination, and we will stay that way. We will have at least three couples whom we would rate as good friends (or better) and a larger number of acquaintances. We will visit our children frequently, but not so often that we intrude or interfere, as indicated by their telling us to leave or asking us more than twice in a row not to come.

Notice that this hypothetical *What-Should-Be* statement:

- Is measurable.

- Identifies who (or what) will display the desired behaviors and attitudes.

- Lists the criteria for evaluation and the conditions for evaluation.

- Leaves little room for confusion.

It also is PEOPLE-CENTERED!

When you are preparing your objectives (or goals), aside from making them MEASURABLE, also remember to talk about

ENDS

not

MEANS, or

How-to-do-its.

Let's see, the statement spoke of self-sufficiency, survival, and contribution, regardless of the INPUTS, PROCESSES, PRODUCTS, and OUTPUTS achieved, so it must be an OUTCOME statement.

If you are getting a certain set of results (PRODUCTS, OUTPUTS, or OUTCOMES) now, and you want to achieve a different or modified set, you should make two parallel lists . . .

a WHAT-IS list and a WHAT-SHOULD-BE list.

Pick an area of interest to yourself and try it out.

And note, please, that results may be
internal and external
and they also relate to
PRODUCTS, OUTPUTS, and OUTCOMES.

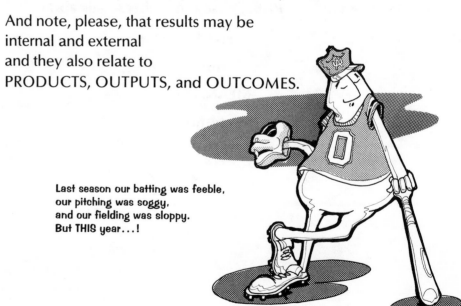

Last season our batting was feeble,
our pitching was soggy,
and our fielding was sloppy.
But THIS year...!

WHAT IS (current results)	**WHAT SHOULD BE** (desired results)
Earning $21,000 a year at age 39	Earn at least $45,000 a year in 16 years
Paying $450 a month principal and interest on house	Pay off mortgage within 16 years
Own one car	Own two cars
Net worth of $4,975.00 (No investment program)	Net worth of at least $100,000 (Begin by putting aside at least $300 a month for income property and other investments)
10% to 15% days per year feeling "sub par." (Sporadic health checks when health is poor)	Feeling physically "sub par" 5% of the time or less per year
	Regular checkups with physician and certification of good health

Check your *What-Is* list and your *What-Should-Be* list against our criteria for a statement of results:

- Do they tell what OUTCOME (or PRODUCT, or OUTPUT) is to be achieved?

- Do they tell when the OUTCOME (or PRODUCT, or OUTPUT) will be achieved and what criteria (measures) will be used to determine its achievement?

- Do they tell by whom and what the achievement will be measured?

- Do they avoid ambiguity and confusion?

(If they don't meet all these specifications, go back and revise them.)

Criteria are most usefully stated in interval or ratio-scale measures.

Results statements, such as this, are called objectives.

You will, probably, have to have more practice writing measurable results statements.

Results statements (objectives) may relate to OUTCOMES, OUTPUTS, and PRODUCTS.

Don't get discouraged or lose interest . . .
The trip is worthwhile.

I'm packed
and ready to go!

Anyway, keep at it.

You've probably had quite enough now.

At least

take

a

S-T-R-E-T-C-H !

Identifying and Solving Problems

Want to take other people into consideration?

Most people aren't alone in the world (although we might feel pretty lonely from time to time), and what we do affects others—and vice versa.

So why not take into account these interactions and interrelationships?

When we are selecting goals and objectives, we can involve our partners in NEEDS ASSESSMENT.

Each partner, or group of partners, can (and really should) fill out a What-Is and What-Should-Be statement.

Let's say you are doing some educational or training planning and you have, at least, the following partners:

Learner or Recipient

Associates: Partners, Co-Workers, Teachers, Administrators

Society: Parents, Clubs, Citizens, etc.

Include a What-Is and What-Should-Be analysis for each group.

	WHAT IS (Results)	**WHAT SHOULD BE** (Results)
Learner		
Associates		
Society		

Remember to make all statements measurable on an interval (or ratio) scale.

Remember, a
NEED
is a gap between

What Is and What Should Be in terms of
RESULTS.

One possible way to keep MEANS and ENDS separate is to list both MEANS and ENDS along with the possible methods and MEANS, as we have them below . . .

What Is (Current Results)	Possible Methods and MEANS To Get from Is to Should Be	What Should Be (Desired Results)

The MEANS are how you meet or reduce a NEED . . . how you get from CURRENT to DESIRED results.

Now the purpose of going through all this is to do a
NEEDS ASSESSMENT

A NEEDS ASSESSMENT is a *formal* analysis that

- Shows and documents the gaps between current results and desired results (ideally concerned with gaps in OUTCOMES).

- Arranges the gaps (NEEDS) in priority order.

- Selects the NEEDS to be resolved.

When you list the gaps between *What Is* and *What Should Be* for you and your partners, you can reconcile any differences (or mismatches) by negotiation, capitulation, manipulation, intimidation, bribery, or just plain, rational reasoning.

Agreement usually is easier when we discuss ENDS, agree on those first, and then discuss MEANS.

NEEDS ASSESSMENT is the first step in improving decision making. It is essential to useful planning. It assures us that where we are going is where we should be going and, further, that our partners agree!

It is

PURPOSIVE,

HUMANE,

and

PRACTICAL.

And I'm beginning to see how it might work.

Before moving from identifying NEEDS to How To Resolve
Them . . .

Here is one more aspect of assessing NEEDS and of
relating NEEDS to *possible* MEANS and resources for
achieving success!

Defining

- WHAT IS

    and

- WHAT SHOULD BE

    for *each* of the

    Organizational Elements.

Let's divide the Organizational Elements further into

- What Is and
- What Should Be!

	INPUTS	PROCESSES	PRODUCTS	OUTPUTS	OUTCOMES
WHAT IS					
WHAT SHOULD BE					

In conducting an analysis, we could move from the precise measurable (in interval or ratio-scale terms) determination of WHAT IS for each element,

and then,

do the same for WHAT SHOULD BE.

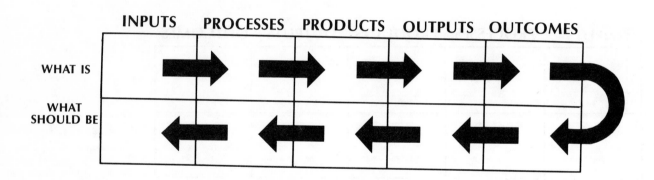

Once we have done that, then we may determine (and justify)
NEEDS:

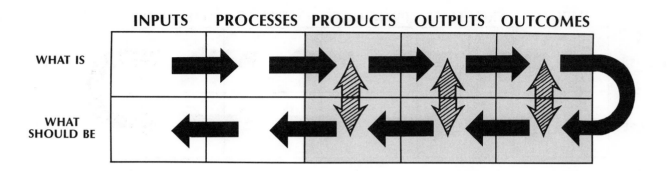

	INPUTS	PROCESSES	PRODUCTS	OUTPUTS	OUTCOMES
WHAT IS					
WHAT SHOULD BE					

Remember?
NEEDS are gaps in
results only!!!

... and we also may determine gaps in INPUTS and PROCESSES:

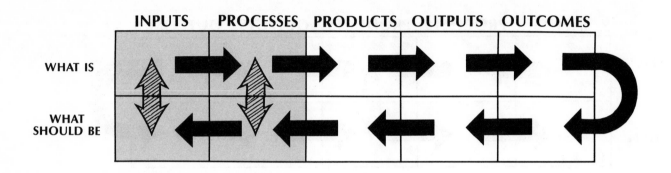

Gaps in PROCESSES as well as gaps in INPUTS are really

QUASI-NEEDS

To complete a rigorous Organizational Needs Assessment, you would determine

- NEEDS

  and

- QUASI-NEEDS

  for each of the
  Organizational Elements

. . . and then, for each Element,
determine

- CHANGE REQUIREMENTS

- CONTINUATION REQUIREMENTS (that which
  should be left alone)

and then you will be able to close the gaps

- IDENTIFYING POSSIBLE INTERVENTIONS and
  how-to-do-it (MEANS)

and then

- SELECTING INTERVENTIONS

Keeping in mind that not all NEEDS and problems arise from a gap *within* an existing system or organization . . .

Sometimes there are gaps in societal results to which no existing organization is currently responsive. A new organization *might* be considered to help close the gaps.

Thus, two assumptions you should *stay away from* are that

"My organization can solve all problems"

and

"Needs are deficiencies, not discrepancies."

What?

Organizations are existing MEANS to societal ENDS. We might want to create new organizations or change some existing ones—based on NEEDS.

Needs Assessment may identify gaps in results, be they *too little* or *too much* of something . . . NEEDS are discrepancies and not necessarily deficiencies.

There are 1 million graduates in law available.

I don't think we can use that many.

Once you have identified, documented, and justified

NEEDS

and

QUASI NEEDS . . .

You are ready to

get from

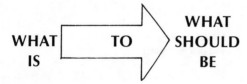

three

how to get from here to there
– the bridge to success

If you've done what was suggested previously you have:

- Listed gaps between current results and desired results,

  and

- Selected NEEDS—those gaps that have the highest priorities.

You know WHERE YOU ARE and
WHERE YOU WANT TO BE.

Now it is time to:

- Perform an analysis to determine all the requirements (specifications) necessary to get from

  HERE $\boxed{\text{TO}}\!\!>$ **THERE**

- Identify possible ways and means to get you there in the quickest and easiest manner so that later you can select the *best* ways and means.

- Assure yourself that the "trip" is feasible.

We are now ready to:

- Shift from the EXTERNAL goals and objectives to INTERNAL goals and objectives,

- Determine the requirements and possible ways and means to get from

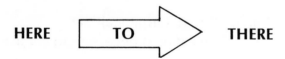

HERE **TO** **THERE**

- Plan and accomplish the INTERNAL goals and objectives.

This builds a "bridge" for getting from CURRENT RESULTS to DESIRED RESULTS—moving from What Is to What Should Be.

The first thing to do is to use your What-Should-Be statement as an overall statement of OUTCOME (or result).

This is called the **MISSION OBJECTIVE.**

This MISSION OBJECTIVE (or overall results statement) should be written in terms of measurable performance:

By July 23, 1990, the Ideal Ice Cream Company (or its surviving organization) will show a positive return on investment, as certified by independent audit, and external success, as indicated by at least a 10 percent increase in per-share stock-market price compared to price one year earlier. In addition, by July 23, 1988, the employees of the Ideal Ice Cream Company will have developed a more positive attitude toward the firm, as indicated by at least a 50 percent drop in absenteeism and employee turnover, a 75 percent reduction in lost orders, and an equal drop in spillage and loading-dock damage as compared to the previous year. There also will be a substantial (at least 70 percent) increase in the number of positive suggestions from employees to management, submitted and used, and a readiness to discuss grievances openly instead of by grumbling in small groups, as measured by a questionnaire filled out by employees. On its side, management will recognize problems when they arise and move to solve them at once without letting them build into major and bitter issues by the time union contract negotiations begin at the end of two years, as measured by a reduction in protracted contract disputes. Management also will take the initiative in instituting an employee recreation program within the next two years.

This sure is long—but I guess it pays to be complete now and avoid misunderstandings later.

From this Mission Objective, next construct a plan—a *management plan*—of what (regardless of *how*—what MEANS are used—to get there) "en-route" PRODUCTS are to be achieved to get you from What Is to What Should Be.

We agree.

That will do it.

That would be fine.

I like the sound of that Management Plan.

CONFERENCE ROOM

The management plan[1] is best shown as a series of PRODUCTS displayed within rectangles that depict the order of, and the relationships between, the en-route PRODUCTS.

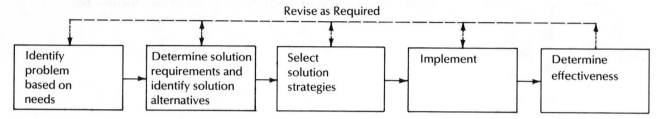

Revise as Required

| Identify problem based on needs | Determine solution requirements and identify solution alternatives | Select solution strategies | Implement | Determine effectiveness |

This is an example of the most general problem-solving process model. Let's take a closer look at each PRODUCT.

The first PRODUCT is to:

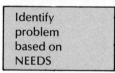

Identify problem based on NEEDS

You have accomplished this when you have identified the gap (NEED) between Current OUTCOMES and Desired OUTCOMES (or any gap in results).

---

[1]See R. A. Kaufman. *Educational System Planning*. Englewood Cliffs, N.J.: Prentice-Hall, 1972.

The second PRODUCT is to:

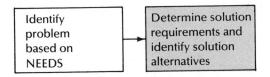

| Identify problem based on NEEDS | → | Determine solution requirements and identify solution alternatives |

Here *all* the requirements for getting from What Is to What Should Be are analyzed, and alternative ways and means to meet these requirements are identified (but not selected).

That's a big job but a sensible way to start getting it done.

And we can better plan and relate the internal efforts and resources.

From your *What-Should-Be* statement (Mission Objective), you then draw a management plan showing each function in your overall plan. The overall plan, called a **MISSION PROFILE**, for identifying and solving *any* problem looks like this:

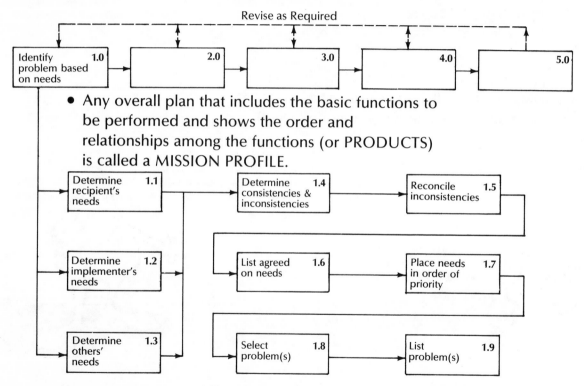

Revise as Required

| Identify problem based on needs 1.0 | 2.0 | 3.0 | 4.0 | 5.0 |

● Any overall plan that includes the basic functions to be performed and shows the order and relationships among the functions (or PRODUCTS) is called a MISSION PROFILE.

Determine recipient's needs 1.1

Determine consistencies & inconsistencies 1.4

Reconcile inconsistencies 1.5

Determine implementer's needs 1.2

List agreed on needs 1.6

Place needs in order of priority 1.7

Determine others' needs 1.3

Select problem(s) 1.8

List problem(s) 1.9

A MISSION PROFILE can be developed for identifying and resolving any problem.

It may be developed for a very comprehensive area (such as this six-step one for identifying and resolving any problem)

or

It may be developed for a very specific problem, such as meeting the MISSION OBJECTIVE for the Ideal Ice Cream Company.

Each function (or PRODUCT) in the MISSION PROFILE has a number with a zero after the decimal point: 1.0, 13.0, 14.0, etc.

A mission profile may be developed to get from What Is to What Should Be for any one (or combination) of the Organizational Elements.

The process of developing a "mini-management plan," or "break-out," is called **FUNCTION ANALYSIS**. Each mini-plan has a number related to its functions, such as: 1.1, 1.2, 1.9, 1.1.1, 1.9.1, 1.9.2, etc. The different names and numbers emphasize differences in levels of planning.

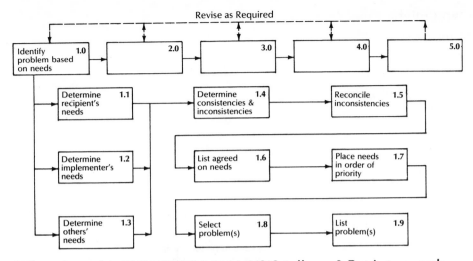

What does this FUNCTION ANALYSIS tell you? Put into words, it says: In order to identify the problem, based on NEED (1.0) you:

1.1   Determine the recipient's NEEDS, and

1.2   Determine the implementer's NEEDS, and

1.3   Determine others' NEEDS, and

1.4   Determine those NEEDS about which there is agreement or disagreement

. . . then

1.5 Reconcile the inconsistencies (you might later elect to negotiate, convince, bully, etc.)

then

1.6 List the NEEDS about which there is agreement,

then

1.7 Place the NEEDS in order of priority,

then

1.8 Select the problem(s) to be worked on (A problem is a NEED selected for resolution), and

then

1.9 List the selected problem(s).

I have to remember that NEEDS are gaps between current results and desired results . . . not PROCESSES or resources.

Next, do a break-out (function analysis) for each element in the overall plan (Mission Profile) on as many levels as necessary to define all the important requirements and interrelationships . . .

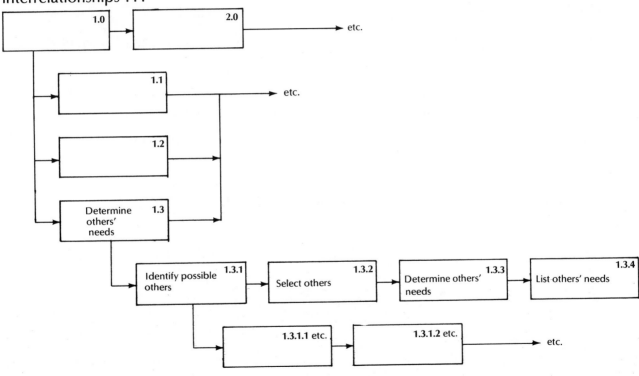

EACH TIME YOU IDENTIFY A FUNCTION

- **List measurable specifications for the accomplishment of each one**

and

- **Identify possible ways and means for meeting each specification.**

The identification of possible ways and means is accomplished without selecting "how-to-do-its"—in order to

CONSIDER ALTERNATIVES

and

KEEP THE OPTIONS OPEN!

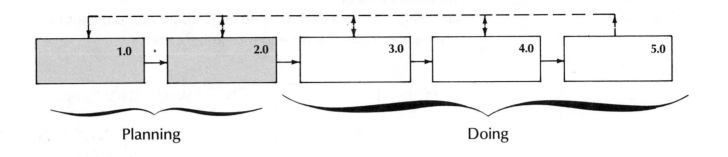

The First Two Steps (1.0 and 2.0)
may be considered to be

PLANNING

and the balance is

DOING.

The Third Product

is to select the most *effective* and *efficient* ways and means of meeting the requirements and thus getting from

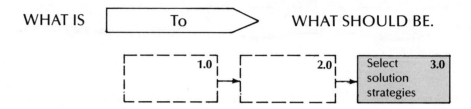

WHAT IS [To] WHAT SHOULD BE.

The Fourth Product

is to do what you planned (in **1.0** and **2.0**) with the ways and means you selected (in **3.0**) . . .

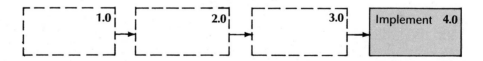

The Fifth Product

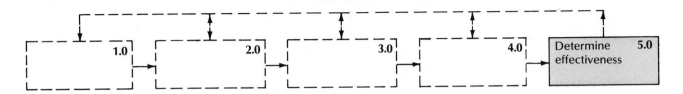

is to determine how well or how poorly the requirements have been met.

You mean I can measure my performance too?

The Sixth Product

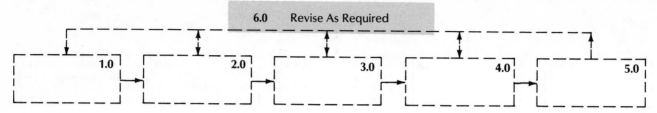

is to make changes any time and any place in your planning and doing process when you are not getting where you want to be—this is a self-correcting process.

Changing as required and when required as you move from What Is to What Should Be is called "formative evaluation."

Changing on the basis of the end-of-program results is termed "summative evaluation."

This six-step problem-solving process is a basic tool that is useful any time you want to identify and resolve problems!

---

[2]See R. A. Kaufman. *Educational System Planning*. Englewood Cliffs, N.J.: Prentice-Hall, 1972.

Let's go back to our original MISSION OBJECTIVE:

By July 23, 1990, the Ideal Ice Cream Company (or its surviving organization) will show a positive return on investment, as certified by independent audit, and external success, as indicated by at least a 10 percent increase in per-share stock-market price compared to price one year earlier. In addition, by July 23, 1988, the employees of the Ideal Ice Cream Company will have developed a more positive attitude toward the firm, as indicated by at least a 50 percent drop in absenteeism and employee turnover, a 75 percent reduction in lost orders, and an equal drop in spillage and loading-dock damage as compared to the previous year. There also will be a substantial (at least 70 percent) increase in the number of positive suggestions from employees to management, submitted and used, and a readiness to discuss grievances openly instead of by grumbling in small groups, as measured by a questionnaire filled out by employees. On its side, management will recognize problems when they arise and move to solve them at once without letting them build into major and bitter issues by the time union contract negotiations begin at the end of two years, as measured by a reduction in protracted contract disputes. Management also will take the initiative in instituting an employee recreation program within the next two years.

With this What Should Be statement, now draw a plan (mission profile) for getting from where you are to the accomplishment you want . . .

This statement has all the characteristics of an objective.

Perhaps it would look like this:

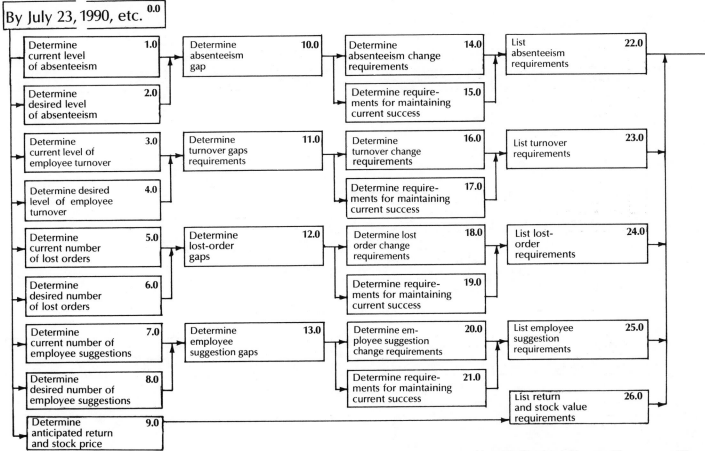

By July 23, 1990, etc. **0.0**

Determine current level of absenteeism **1.0**	Determine absenteeism gap **10.0**	Determine absenteeism change requirements **14.0**	List absenteeism requirements **22.0**
Determine desired level of absenteeism **2.0**		Determine requirements for maintaining current success **15.0**	
Determine current level of employee turnover **3.0**	Determine turnover gaps requirements **11.0**	Determine turnover change requirements **16.0**	List turnover requirements **23.0**
Determine desired level of employee turnover **4.0**		Determine requirements for maintaining current success **17.0**	
Determine current number of lost orders **5.0**	Determine lost-order gaps **12.0**	Determine lost order change requirements **18.0**	List lost-order requirements **24.0**
Determine desired number of lost orders **6.0**		Determine requirements for maintaining current success **19.0**	
Determine current number of employee suggestions **7.0**	Determine employee suggestion gaps **13.0**	Determine employee suggestion change requirements **20.0**	List employee suggestion requirements **25.0**
Determine desired number of employee suggestions **8.0**		Determine requirements for maintaining current success **21.0**	
Determine anticipated return and stock price **9.0**			List return and stock value requirements **26.0**

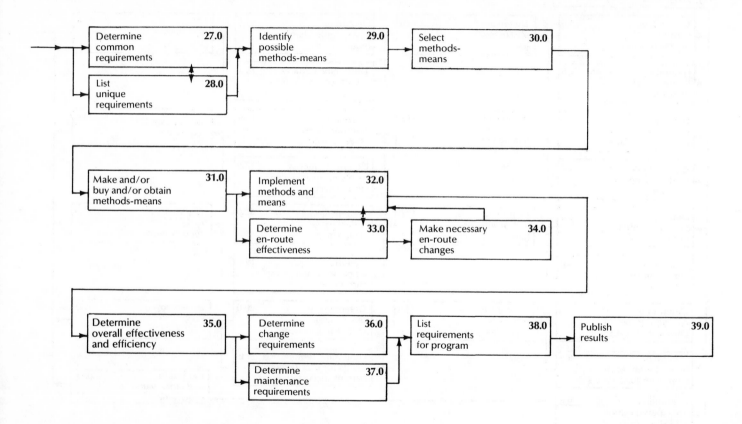

Continue this analysis until you are certain that if you did what you planned you would get from WHAT IS to WHAT SHOULD BE!

Then . . .

Identify possible ways and means for accomplishing each function. Here is a possible (but hypothetical) methods and means analysis for function number **7.0**:

FUNCTION	POSSIBLE WAYS AND MEANS	ADVANTAGES	DISADVANTAGES
7.0 Determine current number of employee suggestions	**A.** Ask top level supervisors **B.** Ask lower level supervisors **C.** Random sampling of employees in each department **D.** Analyze recent contributions to suggestion boxes	**A.** Fast **B.** Closer contact with workers on the floor **C.** First-hand information **D.** Factual	**A.** Too far removed from workers on the floor **B.** Personal bias enters in **C.** Might exaggerate their contributions **D.** Often impossible to tell how many suggestions come from what number of employees; also, some employees reluctant to write anything

This is called Methods-Means Analysis.

You now have the necessary information for *successful* planning:

- An overall objective (mission objective)

- A plan for getting the objective accomplished (mission profile plus function analysis)

- Alternative ways and means for implementing the plan, including a list of the advantages and disadvantages of each

- The assurance of feasibility (if you hadn't found any ways and means, you would know you couldn't do the job)

You are now ready to go from
PLANNING to DOING!

four

decisions, decisions

Some people like to make decisions—others avoid them.

Either way, DECISIONS GET MADE!

Hmmm. I've got to decide
whether I go along with that.

In solving problems with the previous planning and the resulting information, you still have to make decisions—

But now it is

EASIER!

Basically, you can make a wise selection if you

- Know where you are going (mission objective based on NEEDS) . . . and know why you want to go there.

- Know what has to be accomplished to get you from where you are to where you want to be.

- Know the alternative ways and means (how-to-do-its) to get from "here" to "there."

. . . and if you've followed along until now, you have all that information!

Wait a minute!
How do I sort out
all those alternatives?

Making useful decisions simply involves asking (and answering)
two simultaneous questions:

"What do I give?"

and

"What do I get?"

Just relating costs and
results . . . Sounds too
easy. What's the trap?

List your alternative ways and means for doing the job (or getting from where you are to where you want to be) AND select the best ones on the basis of the answer to this question:

What is the highest (or best) payoff for the lowest investment?

(Don't put it off, because
not making a decision…is a DECISION.)

For example:

Alternative	Cost	Result/Benefit
1. Spend vacation visiting our friends the Websters	**1.A.** $75 for travel **1.B.** Sleep on sofa-bed **1.C.** Have to see their tedious friends **1.D.** Have to eat Sally Webster's cooking	**1.A.** Have money left after vacation **1.B.** Get to see old friends **1.C.** Get a partial vacation
2. Go to San Juan	**2.A.** $1355 travel **2.B.** Minimum room & board $150 **2.C.** Nervous when flying **2.D.** Will have to borrow and repay $1,100 **2.E.** Maybe only meet new people I wouldn't want to meet	**2.A.** Vacation will be novel **2.B.** Have good memories **2.C.** Meet new people?
3. Stay home	etc.	etc.

You can see that when you are making decisions about personal goals and objectives, your selection of one option among many may be rather subjective.

When you are in more precise areas like business, science, technology, you can do actual COST/RESULTS studies.

Whether you do a formal analysis (usually more effective and efficient) or an informal one, your DECISION is your first affirmative action step.

You have

- defined where you are and where you want to be,
- identified all the steps to be accomplished,
- identified possible optional ways and means to get you there, *plus* listing the advantages and disadvantages of each,
- selected the most effective and efficient how-to-do-its.

In fact

You have decided to **SUCCEED!**

And that's what it's all about!

five

doing what you've planned-well

So you know what you are going to do and how you are going to do it. Your next job is to

You are now ready for *Operational Planning* and *doing:*

- Make, buy, build (or beg, borrow, or steal) the tools for getting the job done

AND

- Schedule resources—make sure that what you will be using will be ready and there when you have to use them.

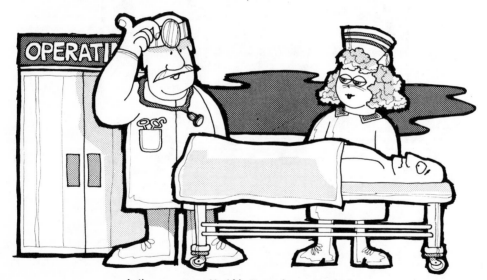

Let's see, nurse. You'd better order one scalpel, a dozen clamps, surgical needle and thread, dressings, one cheeseburger, and...

Some activities are best carried out when we make out a schedule of:

TIME

EVENTS

and/or

INTERRELATIONSHIPS

Some simple schedules consist of a chart (called a Gantt Chart), such as:

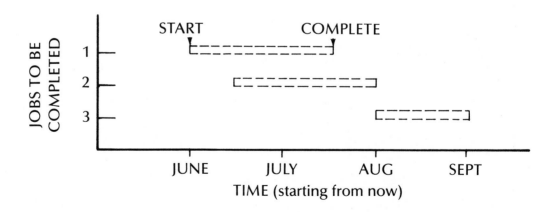

Or a more complex one (called Networks):

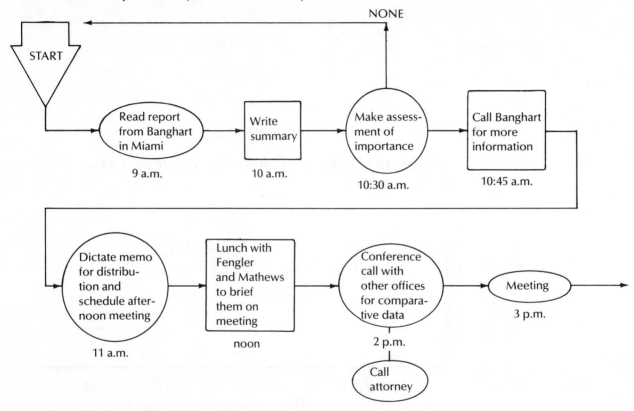

Or a very complex (but usually very useful) one:

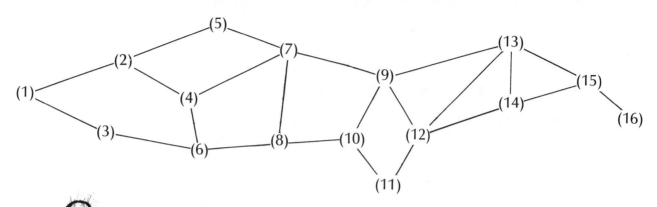

These charts show events, interrelationships between events, and times for each event—and what happens to everything else when some events are early or late.

I've been reading.
This is called PERT—
Program Evaluation Review Technique.

Regardless of how you manage it all, you now are in operation and moving toward SUCCESS, and that requires:

- TIMING

- COMMITMENT

- SENSING AND ADJUSTING

- ORCHESTRATING YOU AND YOUR RESOURCES

Good management for getting from What Is to What Should
Be is

WORKING SMARTER

NOT

WORKING HARDER

That's good life—management too!

six

finding out how you did

Remember, earlier, how much of a fuss we made about
Measurement and **Measurability?**

We stated, in measurable terms, where we were going. Now
the measurable criteria tell us how to know when we've arrived.
We can compare our accomplishment with our objectives.

You mean I can see if I did
what I said I was going to do?

So let's compare by using our Mission Objective from page 94:

Objective	Success or Failure
A) Positive return on investment	A) Success
B) 10 percent share increase in stock	B) Failure
C) 50 percent drop in absenteeism and employee turnover	C) Success
D) 75 percent reduction in lost orders	D) Success
E) Increase in employee suggestions used	E) Failure
F) Management reducing protracted contract disputes	F) Success

This step allows you to see how well or how poorly you have done what you set out to do. In our hypothetical example, we would maintain our performance on objectives A, C, and D and F. We would revise our procedures for objectives B and E. We might question the validity of our gap (NEED) on employee suggestions. Go back to the data collected for functions 7.0, 8.0, 13.0, 20.0, 21.0, 25.0, 27.0, 28.0, 29.0, 30.0, 31.0, 32.0, 33.0, 34.0 (Mission Profile on pages 111 and 112) to assure their correctness and make whatever changes might be necessary.

Evaluation can be your best friend. It can tell:

- Where you were successful
- Where you should make changes— where renewal should take place

While you are solving a problem and when you have completed the problem-solving process, you should always learn from any mistakes. Use the information about the gaps between that which you have accomplished and that which you have not accomplished.

seven

"if once you don't succeed..."

Sad, but true, we aren't always successful in doing everything we set out to do . . .

So your job, both here and throughout, is to

REVISE AS REQUIRED

…whenever and wherever you have not accomplished what you set out to accomplish.

Each time you achieve a result, determine if you are "on target" and, if not, where you should revise.

Because all your objectives are written in measurable terms, you can, at any point, see where you are "off target."

At any step of the process, you should go back and re-do whenever you are not getting from What Is to What Should Be.

THIS PROCESS CAN

ACHIEVE RENEWAL OF THE SYSTEM

You can do a number of things:

- Change the objective(s)
- Find another way to try to meet the objective(s)
- Quit

Usually, changing the objective will result in your NOT meeting the original NEED!

But it is worth checking your NEEDS to make sure that they still are appropriate. Things change fast, and you want to be "on top" of reality constantly.

Most often, you should look for other ways and means to meet your unmet objectives, so move back to the **Second Step.**(it is in the detailed solution requirements and possible alternatives that failures most often may be turned into successes);

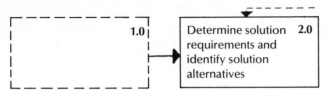

and re-do (or revise) as required.

Every once in a while, you should decide to

especially if the potential payoff doesn't match what it costs to meet the objective.

If you do stop, however, go back to your NEEDS ASSESSMENT and start all over again. In fact, you might want to re-do the entire Organizational Elements Model analysis for all of the What Is's and What Should Be's.

The last step of this problem-solving process (like NEEDS ASSESSMENT) is a constant, ongoing procedure. It is self-correcting in order that your decision to change will better assure . . .

eight

so?
putting the tools to work

You have just hit the

high spots of a PROCESS for successful decision making: a SYSTEM APPROACH to identifying, justifying, and solving problems.

A *System Approach* has two parts:

- One for identifying "What Is" and "What Should Be"—
  determining NEEDS

  and

- One for determining what must be accomplished in
  order to get from What Is to What Should Be.

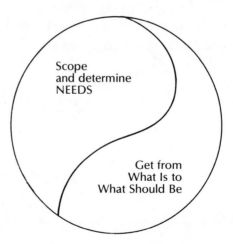

Scope
and determine
NEEDS

Get from
What Is to
What Should Be

The *Organizational Elements Model:*

	INPUTS	PROCESSES	PRODUCTS	OUTPUTS	OUTCOMES
WHAT IS					
WHAT SHOULD BE					

is used to SCOPE the areas of NEED and to document What Is
and What Should Be for Societal Impact, Organizational
Results, and Organizational Efforts.

The six-step problem-solving process . . .

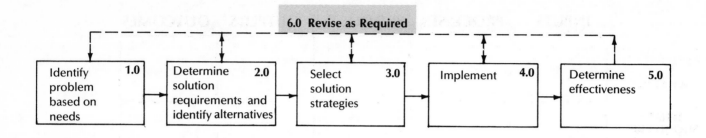

is used to identify *What* must be accomplished in order to
resolve any problem . . . it builds the bridge between What Is
and What Should Be, and thus meets the NEEDS that have
been identified, justified, and selected for resolution.

You may use the six-step problem-solving process for any one
(or combination) of the ORGANIZATIONAL ELEMENTS:

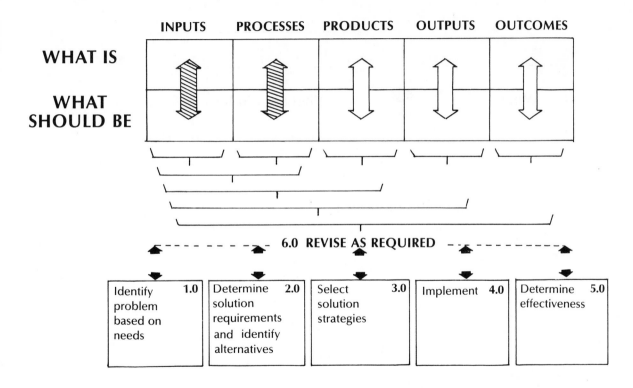

. . . any time you want to determine gaps between

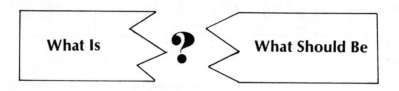

. . . and close those gaps.

The ORGANIZATIONAL ELEMENTS MODEL will allow you to:

- SEPARATE MEANS AND ENDS

- LIST WHAT IS AND WHAT SHOULD BE FOR
  EACH ELEMENT

- DETERMINE NEEDS (gaps in results) TO BE CLOSED

- DETERMINE "QUASI-NEEDS" (gaps in resources or
  methods) TO BE CLOSED

then . . .

the six-step problem-solving process will be a useful tool for:

- DETERMINING A MISSION OBJECTIVE AND SPECIFICATIONS FOR GETTING FROM WHAT IS TO WHAT SHOULD BE

- IDENTIFYING A MAJOR (Mission Profile) MANAGEMENT PLAN PLUS MINOR (Functional Analysis) MANAGEMENT PLANS TO LIST WHAT HAS TO BE ACCOMPLISHED AND IN WHAT ORDER IT MUST BE FINISHED

- LISTING POSSIBLE WAYS AND MEANS TO ACCOMPLISH EACH FUNCTION

and . . .

- SELECTING THE BEST STRATEGIES AND TOOLS

- SHOWING WHAT MUST BE DONE TO SUCCESSFULLY IMPLEMENT THE SELECTED STRATEGIES AND TOOLS

- DETERMINING THE OVERALL EFFECTIVENESS

and, finally,

- REVISING WHEREVER AND WHENEVER REQUIRED.

The ORGANIZATIONAL ELEMENTS MODEL

and

The SIX-STEP PROBLEM-SOLVING PROCESS

together may be used
as partners

To IDENTIFY   and   SOLVE   Important problems . . .

A SYSTEM APPROACH

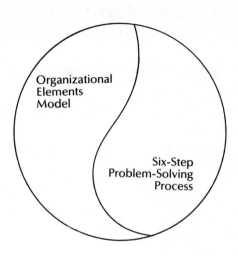

YOUR SUCCESSES WILL EXCEED YOUR FAILURES

IF YOU USE

THE SYSTEM APPROACH

You will see that
your efforts will be:

EFFECTIVE

EFFICIENT

HUMANE

That's "S" for system approach . . .
better than a ROLLS for
getting from here to there.

GETTING IN THE LAST WORD . . .

You now should have some basic concepts and tools for making useful decisions that lead to success.

No idea or concept is useful if it is not put into action, so try these ideas out and see that they work. The tools for identifying and solving problems are available to serve you.

One-shot problem-solving is useful in the short-run. For best results, use these tools continuously to identify and solve problems.

Remember that these processes can be changed and modified to suit your individual situation . . .

And that they will serve you only if you decide to try them.

. . . and he is
on course
now!

REFERENCES

Kaufman, R. A. *Educational system planning.* Englewood Cliffs, NJ: Prentice-Hall, 1972.

Kaufman, R., & English, F. W. *Needs assessment: Concept and application.* Englewood Cliffs, NJ: Educational Technology Publications, 1979.

Kaufman, R., & Thomas, S. *Evaluation Without Fear.* New York: Franklin Watts, 1980.